All for You

(because you deserve so many things)

Written by M.H. Clark · Designed and Illustrated by Jill Labieniec

This book is for you—all for you.

To brighten your day. To send you a smile. And to remind you that the world is full of small delights. If I could, I'd give you all of this and then some. Because you're wonderful. And because you deserve so many things.

You deserve a beach vacation,

Tropical drinks with paper umbrellas,

And a nice long
nap in the shade.

You deserve a perfect latte,

A day off from work,

And a new outfit that
makes you feel fantastic.

(Because you are.)

You deserve a picnic in
a hot air balloon,

With exquisite desserts,

And a gorgeous sunset with
all of your favorite people.

(Because you're
one of mine.)

You deserve a bouquet
of wildflowers,

No, a really big bouquet
of wildflowers,

A letter from a faraway friend,

And a surprise
package with something
sparkly inside.

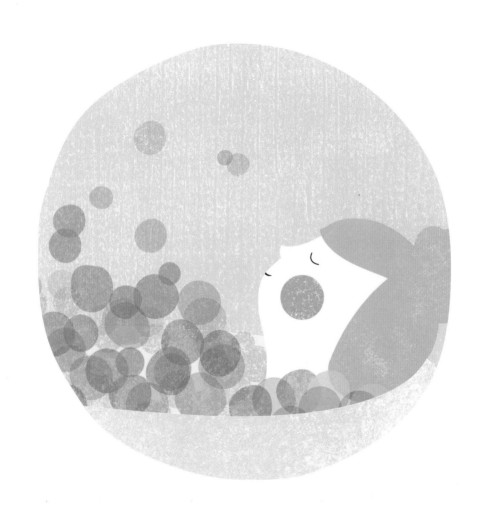

You deserve a bubble bath,

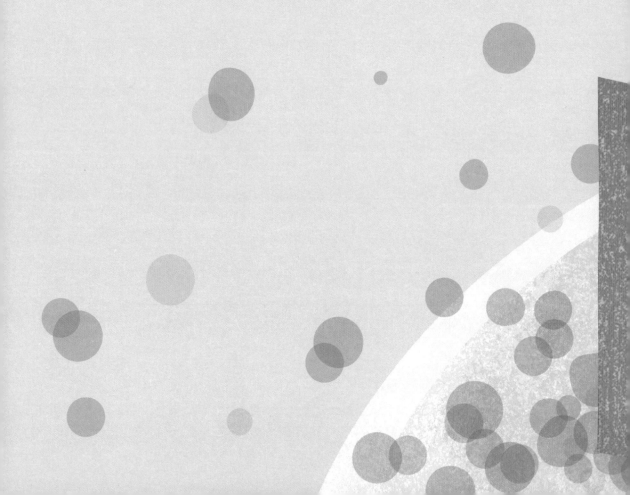

A book you can't put down,

And an hour of complete relaxation.

(Because you're worth it.)

You deserve to dance outdoors
under twinkling lights,

See a shooting star,

And have a wish
come true.

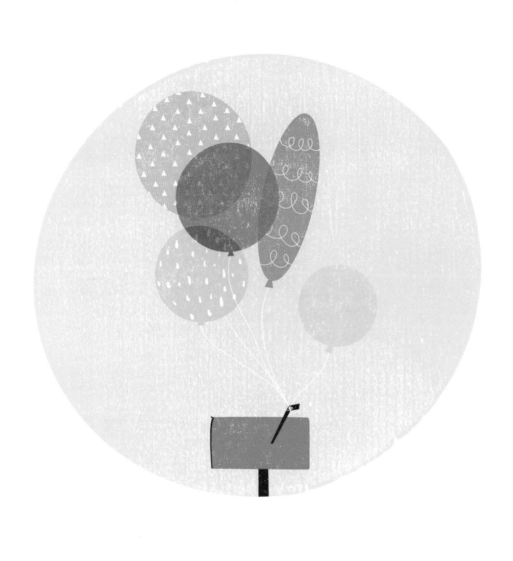

And you should absolutely
know how wonderful you are,

And how much you're appreciated.

You deserve so many
wonderful things. Every day.

All for you.

With special thanks to the entire Compendium family.

Credits:

Written by: M.H. Clark

Designed and Illustrated by: Jill Labieniec

Edited by: Kristin Eade and Amelia Riedler

ISBN:978-1-938298-93-6

1st printing. Printed in China with soy inks.